# MASTERING CONVERSATIONAL CHEMISTRY:

*COMMUNICATE YOUR WAY TO SUCCESS*

# Jose L. Hernandez

Edited by:
Samantha Boesch

Printed in the United States of America

First Printing, 2019

ISBN-13: 978-0-578-53514-2
ISBN-10:  0-578-53514-9

# Table of Contents

# 1. WHAT IS CONVERSATIONAL CHEMISTRY

Conversational chemistry is something we all have to deal with on a daily basis, yet it never seems to get any easier. Some of our conversations go smoothly as if they just seem to flow, but others aren't as simple. Most people are pretty comfortable when it comes to speaking, or at least they feel this way because they speak to the same people every day. But others of us find ourselves struggling with and lacking the confidence needed to communicate with other people. I am sure you can recall times that you froze up, embarrassed yourself, or left a conversation feeling down and dejected.

Conversational chemistry doesn't have to be like this though. In fact, it can be fun, exciting, and incredibly useful for improving your life. However, most of us never get to experience this and reap the incredible benefits that can come from understanding conversational chemistry because we don't have the necessary skills to harness it.

If you've ever been in the situation where you hate yourself for not being able to put the right words together during a conversation, this book is your cure.

This book will teach you exactly how to master conversational chemistry by being able to understand the dynamics of a conversation, so that you can effortlessly converse with anyone you encounter. No matter what the environment is, you will be able to chat with people in a way that not only makes them like you but can massively improve your life.

You will learn everything from the power of conversational chemistry and how to leverage it for success, to decoding the body language of others and making a winning first impression.

You might not know it but understanding and mastering conversational chemistry is one of the fastest ways to improve your life and help you in your career. Want to meet a new potential business partner? Want to explore new business ventures? How about meeting with a new client? Want to climb the corporate ladder? Want to avoid being laid off?

Whatever your goals are, the skill of making simple conversation is essential.

I won't be teaching you to rhyme off random, memorized lines. This book is about learning to make natural conversation that draws people towards you, makes them like you, and has you enjoying different types of conversations with different people.

So, if you've ever wanted to learn the art of conversational chemistry, and have the ability to speak to anyone, anywhere, at any time, then you're going to find this book incredibly life-changing. The intention behind this book isn't to make you think that every conversation you have is going to be the same, or that we all speak the same way. I'm not going to give you hundreds of strategies that contradict each other and take months to learn. Instead, I'll provide you with the simplest and most effective strategies with step-by-step instructions, so that you can implement them right away. I'm looking forward to going on this journey with you and helping you become the best version of yourself. Let's get started!

# 2. LISTENING

It is said that if 50% of a conversation is speaking, the other 50% should be listening, right? Well yes, you need both parts to have an active conversation, but I always say that listening is more important than speaking. It is simply worth more. People often ask me how it can be worth more if it is half of what a conversation entails. The answer is because when you speak, you're handling many different things at once. For example, you're thinking about what you are saying, how you are saying it, who you are speaking with, and the speed in which you are saying it. When you listen, you should only be listening to understand and learn something. It is one of the best ways to show respect.

Hearing is something that just happens. Most of the time it is not something that you are doing, it is something that happens to you. If you only hear a conversation, then you are not really having one. Hearing a conversation is very different from engaging in a conversation.

Distractions, such as a mobile phone,

take away from our ability to interact with people on a more human, personal level. I don't want to drum on about phones too much, but in this day and age, they are proving to be a massive barrier between people in real life. When we try to divide our attention between conversation and phone calls, apps, and other electronic chaos, we lose an opportunity to make a real connection. These connections are an essential part of the human experience, and they are worth more of our time than all of our devices combined.

Let me say that there is no doubt that digital devices are incredible. I absolutely adore mine. These incredible inventions allow us the opportunity to meet people we might never have met without the help of the device. They give us a world of information at our fingertips. However, study after study is showing that the rapid growth of smartphones, especially with younger and younger children, is negatively affecting our actual real-life communication skills. All the apps allowing us to connect with people online are utterly useless if we cannot then communicate with them effectively offline!

As smartphones become even more ingrained in our culture, this trend is sure to increase. Kids today seem to be born already attached to electronic devices. Give any toddler an iPad and just see what they can do. It is quite amazing. Perhaps it is about time we realized that sometimes we just need to unplug for a while.

For many people I have talked to, the smartphone is their go-to safety device. They have told me stories about standing in a bar, even with friends, and feeling awkward as they didn't really know how to join in the conversation. Because of this, the phone usually comes out and throws them even further out of the communication circle. In doing this, you are missing opportunities for genuine human interaction and growth in life.

Listening involves taking an interest in what the speaker is saying. Looking at your phone or around the room is the easiest way to tell the person that you're not interested. You are putting up a wall and letting that person know that you do not really value their opinion. You are unconsciously saying that you are bored and that you don't want to be there.

During a conversation, many factors can distract you, or make you appear distracted. There are a million little things that you can do that take away your focus and let the other person know that you're not listening. Fidgeting and unnecessary jerky movements are a sign to people that they are being ignored. Playing with your hair, scratching your neck, fumbling with your clothes are also all negative signals to the other person. The general rule is if you are fidgeting, you're not listening. Obviously, I am not saying you need to stand completely still like a statue, but you do need to keep your fidgeting to a minimum, especially during a more serious or deep conversation.

So how do you get rid of these distractions?? The first thing to do is to get out of yourself. By that I mean take an interest in the other person in the conversation. Focus your energy on them, and you will see that this pays off. If you take an interest, generally speaking, people will respond to that, and they will pay more attention to what you are saying as well.

To properly take an interest in the other person, and make them the speaker in the conversation, you need to employ a technique that has become a buzzword over the last several years: active listening. I know, everyone talks about it. The phrase is so ubiquitous, it is almost meaningless. But how many people truly know what it means? Here's a little rundown of the principles behind active listening and why it is so important.

At its most basic, active listening is merely taking an interest in what the other person is saying. As the listener, you are continually sending verbal and non-verbal cues to the speaker that you're interested in what they have to say. You smile, you nod, and you (hopefully) engage in the dialogue. It is also essential to read the response of the speaker and act accordingly. Too much of any of those ingredients can be a problem; no one wants to talk to a bobble-head doll, nodding constantly!

Properly engaging in dialogue is essential if we want to be successful in social situations. The question is how do we engage in active listening without annoying people? It is really easy to irritate the other person with this tactic if we do not do it correctly. Too many people think that active listening is automatically repeating everything that is being said to you. It is not. It is about processing what the other person has said and putting your own spin and view on it.

The key to active listening is that you are directly engaging with the other person's words. Whether it is repeating or paraphrasing, you are taking in everything that is being said and communicating to the other person that you are engaged in the conversation. Engage with the other person and ask questions. This is the active part. You are taking action to ensure that you correctly understand the conversation and you are showing the other person that you are interested in what they are saying.

As previously stated, active listening requires us to focus on the speaker. You have to gauge everything you are doing by how the speaker is reacting to your active listening signals. It is great to agree with the speaker, but too much interjection on your part can make the speaker feel uncomfortable. You should make eye contact, but not too much, because eye contact that is too intense can be unsettling. Nodding is an appropriate active listening technique, but if you are nodding as the speaker describes death in the family then you are sending out the wrong message! You need to be engaged and focused. I would even add that it can be dangerous only to mimic the signs of active listening. When you participate in this practice, you are sending out clear social signals. If you are nodding along to hate speech or other rhetoric and not actually listening you may send the wrong message about yourself to the speaker and other people around you. Learning how to read a situation will help you engage in conversation successfully, because ultimately, the main ingredient in active listening is you.

Reading the speaker involves carefully watching their signals. I will discuss this more in the section on body language, but you have to understand the signals the speaker is putting out.

How are they standing? What is their head doing? Where are they looking and for how long? These are all important questions you should ask when trying to read the speaker. The information you gleam from this will allow you to know the best path to take in the conversation.

The dictionary definition of comprehension is "the ability to understand something." When done correctly, active listening should add to your comprehension of the speaker's topic. As you engage more with the dialogue, you will begin to understand more. The more you understand, the more you will be able to say in response, which will lead to successful and flowing communication. If you are unsure about anything that is being said, you can always just ask! Some people think it is rude to ask for clarification, but in reality, it is quite the opposite. Asking for clarification of key points is an excellent way to show that you are listening. On occasion I had asked for clarification even when I understood what the other person was saying, merely to show them I was interested in what they had to say and wanted to know more.

The key to asking for clarification is to ask an open-ended question. These questions allow the speaker to expand on their point and should provide a deeper understanding for the entire audience. I am going to give an example here, but I first want to give you a situation. In the sample questions below, the active listener is trying to gather more information about an incident in the office involving a man named Lenny and a man named Jeff.

Here's the first example:

**"What happened at the office today?"**
In this example, the listener is taking an interest in the person's life and has asked them a question that allows them plenty of space for elaboration. The only fault of the question is that it is not very specific. The listener may end up hearing about her co-worker's lunch, or the latest shipment of pens.

A more specific question would be:

**"What happened today with Jeff and Lenny?"**

The question has gotten more specific, and now the speaker knows exactly what incident the listener is asking about. The danger of getting specific can be seen in this next question.

Here's a negative example:

**"Why was Lenny such a jerk today?"**

This question is technically an open-ended question. It needs more than a yes or no answer from the speaker, but at the same time, it offers a judgment. The listener is leading the speaker. By letting the speaker know that he/she supports Jeff, the listener has changed the answer that the speaker was going to give. A good open-ended question should offer no judgment.

Do not underestimate the power of listening. In all my years of research, I would say this is the thing that many people who suffer from conversation skills do poorly. They do not realize the power of listening, learning, and comprehending, and how it can improve your own life as well as making the other person so much more receptive to you. It really is a win-win situation.

My favorite part of this chapter is that it starts us off with a very common theme that runs through the whole book: we don't always think about everyday communication. Listening doesn't come naturally to everyone. Talking doesn't come naturally to everyone, but we all assume that communicating is a natural process that we should all understand. This book is going to continue to discuss the social interactions that you take for granted, 1 and turn them on their heads so that you can understand them as social processes. Before we move on, here are some things to remember:

- Hearing is not just listening. It is far from that.
- If 50% of a conversation is speaking, then the other 50% is listening
- Your job as the listener is to prove that you are actually listening.
- Multitasking is a myth! Do not believe it!

This may be the first time you have indeed thought about conversation as anything other than an everyday interaction. Let's take a minute to reframe it. Think of it as a social contract. A contract is full of rules and guidelines. The things I am telling you in this book are guidelines that the participants need to follow before they can properly engage in meaningful conversation. When you ignore the guidelines, then you are sending a direct insult to that person and devaluing them and what they are saying. The contract is broken.

# 3. ARE YOU REALLY LISTENING?

People often assume that listening is easy. It's an activity we do every day and one that requires no effort, but it may not be as easy as we think. Many communication problems with other people would cease to exist if listening were really that easy. The truth is that active listening is a skill that does not come automatically, but it can be learned and practiced. When you show interest, understanding, and response to someone, you are giving that person a rare and valuable gift. You are showing them respect, that they matter, and that they have value.

How will becoming a good listener improve your life? For each of the following suggestions, think of a specific situation in which improved listening skills will make a difference.

I will be able to...

- communicate more effectively with my partner

- communicate more effectively with

my children

- be a better friend

- be successful at work

- take in information more effectively

- be a better learner

- ask effective and appropriate questions

- negotiate with others

- be a good decision-maker

- stay calm in difficult situations

- build better relationships

- be more confident in social situations

- handle disagreements

Now, add any others you can think of.

Listening is not a natural process, but hearing is. If you're not hearing impaired, you won't be able to avoid hearing sounds of a certain intensity, whether you want to or not.

For instance, you are not really listening to the loud music blasting from a passing car, but you can't help hearing it. Listening, however, is a choice. You can choose to become a good listener and create situations that encourage others to talk openly and confidently, as well as situations that will help people become secure in the knowledge that their meaning will be heard and understood.

If you feel as if your listening skills are not very good, you are not alone. Some studies have shown that we use only a quarter of our listening potential and take in a quarter of what is said to us. The other three-quarters of what we hear is forgotten, misunderstood, not heeded, or twisted. This means that we tend to forget most of what we hear within hours of hearing it.

Overall, it seems that it is common for us to miss about half of what someone tells us in a conversation. Many misunderstandings are caused by the fact that when we speak, we assume the other person has heard all of what we said. When in fact, there is a minimal guarantee that effective communication has taken place.

It is easy to drift into bad listening behaviors without realizing we are doing so. We get used to interrupting people who say things we disagree with. We switch off when certain people are speaking or jump to conclusions about what someone is going to say. These are bad habits of listening behavior. The first step to replacing poor listening habits with more helpful ones is recognizing the areas in which we could improve.

So, what makes a good listener? Someone who listens to the whole person and the entire message, not just to the words that are spoken. They do not allow the message to become distorted through personal bias and they listen actively, making encouraging responses and checking the messages that they receive.

As you work on building your listening skills, concentrate on replacing the particular unhelpful habits you have identified with more positive responses. Think of the situations in which you find it hard to listen attentively, and set yourself up to look for them. This way you can begin to nip it in the bud and get back on track.

Let's play a game... in my best jigsaw impression possible.

This is a listening game I do in my workshops, but we should be able to get the same effect here. Now, let's pretend that I am a bus driver. I wake up at 7am to get ready for work. My route starts at 8 am, and I live really close to the yard, so I don't have to rush too much. I get to work. I start my bus, and I leave for my route. Now here is when things start to pick up. I get to my first stop, and I pick up three passengers. I tell them good morning, and I continue to my next stop. At my second stop, I pick up another four passengers. Nobody gets off as they all just started their day and we are off again. At the next stop I pick up two more passengers, but this time one also gets off. At the next two stops, we have three passengers get on at each stop, while only one gets off at each stop. Are you with me still? Now we are getting closer to downtown, so it's getting busier. At the next stop, two more passengers get on the bus, and nobody gets off. The following stop, two passengers get off, and no one gets on. Now it is getting close to 10 a.m., and I am getting hungry, so I plan on going on break since I only have a few more stops before I can actually take a break. At the next two stops, two passengers get on, and one passenger gets off at each stop. Now I have gotten to my last stop before I go on break and I have reached the downtown hub. All of my passengers get off of the bus, including myself to go on a quick break and eat something. Now, if you can tell me how many passengers are on the bus or were on the bus before they all got off, that's great! You were really listening! But that wasn't the question I was going to ask. My question for you is, do you know how many stops the bus made?

We have been programmed to think and focus on what we feel is the most vital information to listen to. We have to learn not to be afraid to ask what we should be focusing on, and not assume what the most important information is. Doing this can help us avoid miscommunication and show our speaker that we are actively listening.

# 4. 2-SECOND RULE: THINK BEFORE YOU SPEAK

I mentioned in the previous chapters that people like talking about themselves. That couldn't be truer. The reason why we all love this is that we just love being heard. When somebody is listening to what we have to say, we feel like we matter. It's not that we like to brag (although, there is nothing wrong with a little of that every now and then). The thing is – people need validation. We are all looking for others to validate who we are and what we do. People love being in the spotlight. Even those that say they don't like talking about themselves usually do that because they've not established an adequate level of trust with others and are afraid that they will receive criticism instead of validation.

Ever heard someone say, "They stole my thunder?" When somebody is in the center of attention, those that feel neglected will try to take the spotlight away from them. Some people are craving attention so much that they always try to make the story about them.

A good conversation involves the spotlight going back and forth, just like the ball in a tennis match. You should share your opinions and experiences, especially if the other party asks you to, but you should also make sure to listen to what they have to say attentively. When the other participant is talking, make sure to let them know that you are listening. Don't make a mistake by rudely interrupting them and jumping in as soon as they finish their sentence.

Is it considered rude to speak as soon as the other party stopped talking? It can be because your conversation partner could have the impression that you couldn't wait for them to finish. They may believe that you didn't listen attentively since you were so eager to start talking. Remember, people like to be heard. The speaker may feel that you were more worried about what you were going to say next than listening to what they were actually saying. Our brains process what we are hearing, and we begin to plan how we will respond. You can't do both effectively at the same time. Take your time.

Fortunately, conversation experts have a solution for this. We call it the "two-second rule." The rule is pretty self-explanatory. It means that you should wait for two seconds before saying anything after the other party finishes speaking. This is especially important if the other participant was speaking for a more extended period of time, or about something that is considered personal. Why should you do that? It will show that you are acknowledging what your conversation partner has just said. Two seconds is considered an appropriate amount of time to soak in the information you received.

Where does the idea for the two second rule come from? Our minds can process dozens of words a second, and some studies have even shown more. However, some have said that we can only think as fast as we can speak. Personally, I disagree with that statement. Have you ever seen a listener flip an insult to their advantage so fast that it left the speaker speechless? This is wit. Think about it, this is how you and another person can have a conversation and not sound completely crazy. You sound coherent. You are processing what you are going to say before you say it.

Did you ever hear from your teachers or parents growing up that you need to think before you speak? I have this firm belief that if we pause for two seconds and think about what we are going to say before we say it, we can process fast enough to figure out what we are going to say and how the receiving party might take it, and therefore adjust before we speak. If you think about it, two seconds is nothing but a fraction of a moment for you to gather your thoughts before you put them out to the world, never being able to take them back again. Being able to process that many words in our minds before we say them should allow us the ability not only to think about what we are going to say, but how the person or audience whom we are speaking with will take it. This gives us the opportunity to change what we are about to say if we need to.

You might think that you have a perfect reply or comment to continue the conversation. In most cases, you just can't wait to seize the spotlight and give the perfect response. A wiser thing to do is to wait for two seconds, as it will increase your likability and will send a message that you are genuinely interested and attentively listening.

Two seconds is all it takes to convince people that you are listening to them with attention. Remember, we all love to feel heard when we are speaking. Two seconds seems like a short period of time, but it's just the right amount of time to send a message to the speaker. They will feel that you've given enough thought to what they were saying before you offered a reply. You will make yourself a valuable participant in the conversation by making the other participant feel equally as valuable in the discussion.

In some cases, people can take a short pause during a long story. This pause does not mean that they are finished speaking. Instead, they are just taking a little break. Imagine if you jumped in and interrupted them with your comment, even though their story hasn't been finished. It would immediately decrease your likability, and you would be considered rude. Not to mention that they can think you don't have enough respect for them and even wonder if you ever even cared what they had to say in the first place.

You may ask, how do I fill the two seconds? You can make a brief comment like, "Wow, that's interesting!" This is an example of a sentence you can use to fill the two-second void. Beware of one thing – if you do this too often, it can get annoying. Your conversation partner might also think that you just used the sentence to stop them from talking and seize the spotlight for yourself.

There is a much better way. Think about waiting for two seconds and then starting your response by saying, "that's interesting." Believe it or not, conversation experts have concluded that this improves the efficiency of the two-second rule. By combining the two, you will show the speaker that you acknowledged what they had to say and showed your appreciation for it.

You can try counting two seconds in your head. If it takes you three, no one is going to look at you like you're crazy. Try repeating something they just said to you in a question form. People would look at you looking for signs if you were listening. Repeating something back to them will buy you more time to think about what you are going to say and show that you were listening to them. Also, your facial expression means a lot, so try to look them in the eye if possible, and if they are saying something that might seem either false or crazy, give them the benefit of the doubt. Remember people want to know they have been heard.

As you can see, two seconds can make a big difference in what kind of impression you will leave. That is why you should make sure to apply this conversation tactic and send the right message.

# 5. ARE YOU APPROACHABLE?

Consider where you are in your life right now. Are you a recent graduate going into the workforce? Are you new to sales? Are you new to management? When meeting people for the first time, the best impression you can make is to appear relaxed, confident, and ready to engage. You want to be someone that others want to connect with. This is generally easier said than done, especially when you're nervous, but there are some simple strategies to accomplish this.

When you meet someone for the first time, they judge you on what they see because they have nothing else to go on. So when they see someone who can't or won't make eye contact, who appears fidgety, doesn't smile, and doesn't look like they want to be there, they'll dismiss you without a second thought. Many of these behaviors are culturally transmitted, meaning that the other person is probably not aware that they are judging you, but they are nonetheless, so don't think you can skip this step.

We are going to be covering strategies for making eye contact, genuinely smiling, promoting the correct body language, and a few simple mind hacks you can use to open the small-talk door by always making a great first impression.

If you have difficulty making eye contact, try lightly focusing on the person's ear, or to a point just behind their head. This will make it appear as if you are looking them in the eye, when you are not. It's just a way to trick your brain into doing something it's not comfortable doing. If you feel confident enough to directly look into someone's eyes, then make sure you follow these steps not to appear too intense or creepy. Look into their eyes but don't stare. Blink naturally. Make natural breaks in the eye contact. Don't continually look into their eyes. Break contact roughly every three-four seconds by glancing away.

Fidgeting is a sign of nervousness, and not only does it reduce your appearance of confidence, but it also makes others feel uncomfortable. A simple way to avoid fidgeting is to find something to hold that's appropriate to the situation. If there is nothing to hold then just lightly clasp your hands in a relaxed grip – a tight grip promotes nervousness, and others will subconsciously pick up on this.

Smiling and relaxing are tougher to do convincingly because you will look fake if it isn't natural. Giving someone a fleeting two-second smile, then going back to a straight face tells them that you'd rather count the dimples on a golf ball than talk to them. And if you're not relaxed, you'll look nervous and uncomfortable. The key to being able to smile naturally is to enter a relaxed, positive state.

Know what changes your state of mind. Try listening to your favorite music, replay the memories of happy events from your life, or even use prayer. Triggering these emotions will result in your brain associating those feelings with your current situation. Harness these feelings and before you know it, you will be smiling naturally without consciously knowing it.

Another mighty psychological hack for "saying" the right things with your body language and filling yourself with confidence is to practice power posing. Popularized by Amy Cuddy in her famous

TED Talk, power posing is a simple 1-2-minute exercise that has incredible results on your confidence, happiness, and even cognitive functioning. I highly recommend that you check out her TED Talk, but if you don't have time here is a quick primer on how to power pose.

Before an event that you're feeling nervous about, just go somewhere quiet (like a bathroom stall) and strike a power pose. A power pose is any standing position that represents a powerful stance. A classic example is the superhero pose – hands on your hips, chest out, head held high, and a feeling of dominance. This may sound ridiculous, but the research behind it is outstanding. Try it just once, it only takes 1-2 minutes, and you will feel the difference instantly.

The physical space you occupy also plays a role in the impression you signal to people. You're going to want to pay particular attention to personal space and touching. In a business setting, most people are okay with a handshake and not much more than that. For standing distance, one arm's length has generally considered the boundary here. It's close enough that you can hear, but not so close that you're making the other person feel crowded.

In a more informal setting it's okay to move a bit closer, but let the other person set the distance. If you're the touchy-feely kind, you definitely want to tone it down, and if you have issues with people touching you, remember that you will be sending nonverbal messages about that, so take note as it will impact your approachability.

Finally, take note that the best impression you can make is to be yourself. People like and respect genuineness, and they especially appreciate sincerity. If you try to shy away from who you naturally are, hiding your passions and your personality, people will feel something is "off" about you. They may not be able to place their finger on exactly what it is, but there will be a feeling they just can't quite describe. I'm sure you've personally experienced this before when meeting new people.

It is also exhausting to be someone you are not. Trying to keep up with that personal character is too complicated, and eventually you will slip and show who you really are. Avoid this by being yourself. It is a much more joyous way to go about your life. So, own who you are, be proud of it, and be genuine! If you do this then conversations will flow with ease, people will warm up to you, and find you very approachable.

Sitting down when you are going to speak with someone is another technique of approachability that shows the other person that you value their time and their company. It shows them that you are comfortable and in the moment. When we stand, we seem like we are anxious to leave. This is something my wife was trained on when she became a nurse. You can go into a patient's room and sit for two minutes and chat when you first start your shift, and it will feel longer than standing there for the same amount of time. Think about when you go into your boss's office, for example. Taking the time to sit down will show that you need a moment of their time to speak about something essential versus just walking in mentioning something quick and getting back to work.

I remember an amazing boss I used to have. I remember every time I would go into her office when I needed something, she would always make good eye contact, take her hands off the keyboard, and ask me to have a seat. Talk about feeling appreciated. She literally stopped everything she was doing and gave me all of her attention. This was an excellent experience for me, and something I have incorporated in my daily life because I know how it made me feel, and I would want someone that works with me to feel the same level of respect. On the same note, I have had those bosses that when you walk in, they say, "Hey, what's up," while never looking away from the screen, and still typing while I am talking. How do you think I felt when I came to them for something I needed help with? Sitting down and giving someone your attention plays a significant role in how they will see you.

When I was running my own landscaping business, I had a customer who would always stop me outside when I was working just to see how things were going. I had been doing work for her for quite a while, so we knew each other well at this point. She knew about my kids and wife, and the vacations we took as a family. She was the sweetest old lady you could come across. One day while I was working, she came out to say hello. We started talking, and I could tell she wasn't feeling well. I invited her to have a seat, and we spoke on her patio for about five minutes. She then told me to go ahead and get back to work, but as I was about to get up and leave her, she grabbed my hand and said "Jose, I love that you take time out of your busy day to for a little chit-chat with an old lady like me. The last guy that worked for me always seemed so rushed and never spoke to me like this." That moment hit me hard because this woman had gotten me so much work from her referrals. I cannot even begin to imagine how much work I would have missed, all because she enjoyed our five minutes of sitting down and talking.

# 6. HOW TO INITIATE A CONVERSATION

Initiating a conversation is sometimes the hardest part of having one. I have heard many people say that they try to avoid being the one to start the conversation because it means that they have to keep it going. This is only part of the struggle, and there are a few other things to consider. We need to find someone to talk to, have a reason for engaging in a conversation with them, and find something to talk about.

When you're in a situation where small talk is essential, the first thing to pay attention to is body language. Since most people show approachability through their body language, it's usually not difficult to tell whether someone would prefer to be approached or left alone. For example, someone reading a book on the bus is probably going to want to be left alone, but someone who is looking out the window or just sitting there quietly making eye contact may welcome conversation.

When you approach a potential new

client or a vendor, you want to try and initiate a conversation that starts off on a positive note. I try to always start with a compliment. It helps people to lower their guard, and it makes people feel really good. I remember visiting with a new client for the first time, and I chatted with the receptionist for a few minutes. I gave her a compliment on this very nice clock she had on her desk. When I was speaking with my new client, she mentioned that the receptionist had said I was very nice and that she enjoyed speaking with me. We have to remember that anyone you speak with can lead to someone you may do business with. Treat everyone the same and you will be more successful and have better conversations in the long run.

Many people are afraid to initiate conversation because they don't want to be embarrassed, which comes back to the social anxiety we discussed earlier. People fear being judged and rejected. They don't want to say something offensive or make the other person uncomfortable, so they "play it safe" and don't say anything. This is not a healthy approach because the "play it safe" method is merely an excuse not to overcome the fear of making small talk. Not crushing this fear means they miss out on some great opportunities to meet people, form new relationships, and improve their lives, both in their careers and their personal lives.

Let's start from the very beginning. To have a conversation, you will need to start one. You might think that this is the hardest step of the entire process, but you can make it very easy by applying the advice from this chapter.

It is going to be much easier to start a conversation if you feel confident. Think of it like this, when you are in a meeting in a room full of strangers, the chances are that they feel exactly like you. They may even be more shy and self-aware! How can you become more confident so that you can start a conversation? Begin by talking to your friends and the people you already know. See how easy it is to initiate a conversation with them, and then think about why it's harder with strangers.

Your goal in a crowd of people should be to look outgoing, confident, and calm. Believe, truly believe, that you are a master of starting a conversation. That's what all alpha males (and females) do. You've undoubtedly heard that body language plays a significant role on how people react to you. Three things you want to apply in any situation to achieve confident body language are: a natural smile, good posture, and your arms uncrossed.

You can't just say hi and think you started a conversation. That is just a greeting. It needs to be followed by something to engage the other party. By applying these simple techniques, you will send a message that you are confident, secure, and approachable. On the plus side, you'll appear cheerful, and who doesn't like someone with a happy spirit? But be careful, there is a time and a place. For example, I'm not saying laugh out loud at a business meeting. It's important to adjust your attitude in accordance with where you are.

It is almost common sense if you think about it. When you smile, it is contagious and sends a positive signal out into your surrounding environment. When you smile, the people around you, even strangers, often smile back. When you scan a room full of people, those with a smile on their face will look more like conversation material than the ones wearing a frown.

It's nothing new that you need to be polite, but I'm talking about adjusting your behavior to the social situation you are currently in. A polite approach in business means that you should introduce yourself and shake hands with the other person(s). On the other hand, you might skip this at a party and start the conversation with a witty remark. It really depends on the circumstance you find yourself in. Of course, you should always make sure not to be interruptive or rude. According to an article on Business Insider from 2013, we only have a 7 second window upon meeting someone for them to form an impression about us. That impression is finalized within the first minute, and it is tough to change it afterward. This is why you need to show the nicest and best part of you for a first impression.

Don't think that the job is over once you pull through the introduction line. Make sure to listen carefully to what your conversation partner has to say, and reply with an appropriate response. You need to send a message that you are interested in having the conversation. So make sure you do things like stay focused and make sure not to wander around with your eyes. Furthermore, if you carefully listen to what the other side has to say, they might provide an opportunity to continue the discussion.

If you want to approach a stranger, observing them first might provide you with topics for starting a conversation. Imagine that you are at a party or a networking event. Notice what the other person drinks and initiate a discussion about that drink. If you are at a business meeting, you can use business topics to start a conversation. For my men out there, don't be afraid to compliment another man on his outfit. I take pride in my suits when I dress up, and when someone notices this, it is automatically a positive interaction. I also have a thing for watches, so when people notice my watch it's an easy conversation starter.

Let's discuss some examples from real life that can help you find a way to start a conversation. A commonly used phase is, "Such a nice day, right?" This is not a good conversation starter. It doesn't lead to additional questions or a meaningful conversation. So, what should you talk about? The important thing to know here is that people love to talk about themselves. You need to find a conversation starter that will allow your partner to express their opinion. If you are in a big room full of people, you can use something like, "Hi, I'm (insert name). I'm still not entirely comfortable with this big group of people. How are you handling the situation?" Not only have you asked the other person to talk about themselves, but you also asked for help, which is another great conversation starter. It breaks the ice and shows that you are not afraid of being yourself and being honest.

In any social situation related to business, always keep the hierarchy in mind. There is a big difference between talking to your superiors and talking to your inferiors. Regardless of your conversation partner, make sure to keep your focus on the final goal of the discussion. You want to be kind to your employees, but you want to look and sound like their leader at all times. On the other hand, if the conversation partner is your *superior*, make sure to show them respect.

For example, you may be interested in how to ask your boss for a raise. When doing this, never start with a direct question. Instead, ask for an opinion on your performance. Depending on the answer, you might ask for an increase immediately or explain that you will try to improve your performance in the future to deserve it. Have you ever felt like you wanted to ask for a raise? According to a survey done by PayScale, two thirds of people that ask for a raise get it. Now I am not saying go in tomorrow and ask your boss for a raise if this isn't something you've had time to think through. There are a lot of things to consider here and a conversation like this should be taken seriously. How long have you been there? Are you performing above what is expected? How is your standing with the company as far as attendance and production? You want to make sure you are worth it and aren't asking just because you want more money and feel entitled to it.

Earlier we discussed how a compliment is a great way to start a conversation, which is a great way to break the ice. This isn't the only way, though. Questions are another great way to start a conversation, since they spark interactions that automatically draw in the other person. More specifically, open-ended questions are best because they generate longer responses and give conversational threads to grasp onto. For instance, if you ask, "What was the best part of your day?" the person might say, "I got a mint chocolate chip ice cream from Baskin Robbins. It reminded me of when I was a kid and how I would go there every Sunday afternoon with my family." From this point, you have several conversational threads to grasp on to including: ice cream, Baskin Robbins, childhood, family time, or how you haven't had ice-cream in months and you miss it. The point is that open-ended questions are better for conversations than "yes" or a "no" questions. They require expanded answers or explanations, which then give you an opportunity to take the conversation in a direction that you feel more comfortable with.

Generally, you don't want to begin conversations with "why" questions because, as mentioned before, it tends to put people on the defense. It can sometimes come off as insulting or judgmental, like you are trying to put them down. For example, if you say,

"Why are you staring at your drink?" it has a certain type of negative energy. But, if you want to ask a "why" question, there are two types of strategies you can use. The first would be the curious statement: "I'm curious, why are you staring at your drink?" The second would be to change your choice of words to, "What made you want to..." or "How come..." If you want to soften the statement, you can combine the two. For instance, "I'm curious, how come you're staring at your drink?" All of this has to do with the words we choose. It is as simple as adding a few words or changing some to make your question sound completely different, thus taking away the negative energy.

Another thing that can be a game changer in using questions in conversation is using the power of a first name. Believe it or not, people love to hear their own names. Don't you like to be addressed by your name? When you address people by their name, you increase the chance that they will listen. Plus, they feel like they are important enough for you to have remembered their name. On top of that, you can also create a more casual atmosphere for the conversation by addressing the other party directly. If the person you are engaging with in conversation has a name tag, it is there for a reason. Use it! Again, one of the most empowering things you can do for someone is to use their name because it makes them feel important. When the person doesn't have a name tag, and you introduce yourself, make sure to use their name right way after they give it to you. This not only makes them feel good, but it helps you remember their name to recall later. For example, you just met with a new potential client or even a boss at an interview. They are probably going to shake your hand and say, "It's a pleasure to meet you. I am John Smith." I would respond instantly with, "Mr. Smith, it is a pleasure to meet you. I am Jose Hernandez." Now, nine times out of ten they will tell you that there is no need for the Mister title. This gives you another chance to use their name again and say, "Well, then we can stick to John." This tactic will help you remember their name and show a great deal of respect to the person you have just met. So remember to use the other person's name as quickly as possible, and if they have a unique name, don't be afraid to ask them how to pronounce it. I can almost assure you if you are asking them for clarification on how to pronounce it correctly, you aren't the first person to do so.

# 7. SPEAK POSITIVITY

Positive emotions are the hallmark of a happy person. But interestingly, most people are hard-pressed to develop a positive emotional state. We live in a society where we deal with countless stressors, and staying positive can be very difficult. This negative energy tends to come out in our communication, whether it's with those around us or ourselves. Many times we are unaware that this negative energy is encircling us. Let's discuss some techniques that can help you produce positive energy and improve your communication.

I'm sure you've all heard the saying, "Count your blessings." Have you ever wondered why this is such a popular phrase? It's because we all need to work on being more grateful. I once heard Tony Robbins talk about how we should all start our day with an attitude of gratitude. When you start your day by being grateful, you instantly begin in a positive state. Tomorrow when you wake up, try thinking of some things you're grateful for. Start your day with three minutes of gratitude, but keep in mind that three minutes may seem like an awful lot on the first day. You can start by being grateful for little things such as having a nice bed to sleep in, or having food to eat for breakfast. Build up your gratitude to the bigger things, like the fact that you woke up with air in your lungs, or for your family and your work. When you start your day in a mentality of gratitude, it is harder to let the negative things get you down. It's both extremely common and incredibly easy to get consumed by negativity when we take our blessings for granted, so it is important that we start to change the way we think.

Along with being ungrateful for the things in your life, the habit of complaining also brings negativity to your life. Constantly complaining rarely results in progress. Instead, it demonizes people and promotes resentment. A person who complains is likely to have entitlement issues which greatly affect the people around them. If you're reputed to be a complainer, people will almost always work to avoid you. In such a situation, it becomes difficult to find collaborators for any activity, and the isolation will make you stew in negativity.

That's why most complainers seem to be of the mindset that the universe – and everything in it – is against them. When you resist the urge to complain, you will have more energy, and negativity won't have a chance to consume you. Negative energy is stronger than positive energy, and that is just the truth. It is easier for one negative person to enter a room full of positive people and lower their energy than it is for a positive person to be surrounded by negative people and make them happy. It is just the way it is. So the more you actually try to be positive, the better it will be for you and those around you.

I want you to think of a time when someone showed you genuine appreciation. Perhaps for something you didn't think was such a big deal. Years ago, I was riding in an elevator to go to a business meeting. A woman walked in after me and I said, "Good Morning." She replied with the same greeting and smiled. I then complimented her teal-colored dress. She said thank you and proceeded to tell me how the color teal makes her happy and brightens her mood. I agreed with her, because that is also how I feel about the color teal. Our conversation lasted about 30 seconds. As she got off of the elevator she said, "Thank you, it's great to start my day by hearing someone say something nice. You made my day!" It was hard to believe that I had made her day by simply appreciating something about her and expressing it. What I don't think she realized is how she made me feel as well. I really appreciated the fact that she thanked me for giving her a  compliment. Showing appreciation makes someone else feel good, and this feeling can linger for hours or even days. It can elevate almost anyone's state of mind. Next time you're with someone, try to show appreciation, even in the simplest way possible.

Another way to spread more positivity in your life and the lives of others is to be kind! This should go without saying, but it is clearly something that is affecting our society on a significant scale. My son's elementary school has a massive campaign about being kind. I don't know what happened, and I know that social media has made communicating in some aspects more difficult, but it really is quite simple. In today's world especially, we all need to remember to just be kind and to say nice things. Think about those compliments we have been talking about and give them out freely and with honesty. The opportunities to practice kindness are virtually endless. There are so many people from different backgrounds who are in need of help. People may come to you looking for help, or you may go out there purposely to offer aid. When you lend a helping hand, it makes you feel good about yourself. It helps fight away any negativity you might be harboring. Kindness helps people connect in a much more powerful way. For instance, compared to walking up to a stranger and starting a conversation, it is easier to talk to and interact meaningfully with a person that you just helped.

Have you ever had someone respond to you or reach out to you in an angry manner? Perhaps you yourself have responded angrily when you didn't mean to. There are times when things are going to make us angry, but we have to learn to control our emotions, especially anger. Earlier we learned about the "two second rule", and this is a great way to apply it. Before you say something to someone, stop for a moment and think of how you are going to respond. You could save the situation rather than making it worse. A while back I had an appointment at a tire shop, and when I walked in to ask a question, the guy at the front desk snapped at me. I paused for two seconds and said, "I apologize if I have done something wrong, but I was only asking about my truck." He took a deep breath and let me know that he had just finished a very frustrating phone call with one of his vendors. He apologized and ended up giving me a discount. I could have blown up on him for the way he treated me, but that wouldn't have made my day any better, or his for that matter. Oftentimes, people lash out because they make the mistake of taking out their anger on the wrong person. The next time this happens to you, take two seconds and think before you respond.

There will be times when you end up rubbing people the wrong way. It's inevitable, we can't please everyone. When it happens, have the heart to offer an apology. This doesn't mean that you're weak or at fault, it only means that you intend to get along well with others. Understand that negative emotions are not only triggered from within us, but also from the reactions of other people. When you offer an apology, it means that you're interested in making things work. Doing this could make the offended party less likely to react in a manner that might set off your negative thoughts. Apologizing promotes reconciliation and, by extension, positivity. This comes down again to our ego and our pride. I have witnessed times where people can be so hard headed that even though they know they are wrong, they won't apologize. This doesn't help anyone and can ultimately push people away. Be the bigger person, swallow your pride, and extend a genuine apology. I promise you it isn't going to hurt you and can prevent a lot of future frustration.

Another idea to squash negativity is to laugh as much as you can. There have been medical studies done that show the connection between laughter and increased well-being. Laughter reduces the stress hormone cortisol and promotes the secretion of endorphins in the brain. These feel-good hormones relax a person physically and puts them in a great mood. When you experience negativity, some of the emotions you battle with include anger, anxiety, and irritation, but laughter can make the bad feelings disappear in an instant. There are endless opportunities for tapping into laughter to fight off negativity. For example, if you had been working on a project that eventually tanked, finding something to laugh about in relation to the project might help you move on. There are always going to be things that don't go as planned or as smoothly as you'd hoped. But being able to find a way to keep a light heart about it and throw in some humor will significantly improve the morale of your team and ensure that you are a pleasure for other people to work with.

We also take in negativity all around us. We can fight this by consuming uplifting media as often as we can. Media has a great effect on our state of mind, and if we spend a lot of our time listening to or watching negative entertainment, it will leave us with a bad taste in our mouths. Bad messages have a way of penetrating your mind and seeding negativity. Thus, you should feed your mind with media that entertains and uplifts you, without setting off negative emotions. Develop a taste for the kind of music, books, and movies that lift you into a positive mood. And anytime you feel haunted by negativity, all you'll have to do to feel well again is to consume your favorite entertainment.

Making friends with positive people is an excellent way to stay positive throughout your life. They say that you are the average of the five people you spend most of your time with. And so, if you'd like to have positive thoughts, you might want to seek friends who have bright and positive outlooks on life. This is because habits have a very big impact on your life. When you have friends who are just like you, you can create an environment where you help each other. Also, you won't feel pressured to conform to superficial standards considering that you're already alike. Such a lifestyle allows positivity to thrive.

And finally, do the things that make you happy. There's fulfillment in pursuing the things that make you truly happy, and less so in chasing superficial things that might give you more money or status. This philosophy cuts across all aspects of life. For instance, choose a career that you have a personal reason for wanting or a business that is in your circle of competence. Positivity rains down when you have a good reason for what you do.

Transform your negative energy. I have worked many years in sales. I know that the negative energy can be extremely potent. It can drag you down through the bottomless pit of obsessive thoughts. At the onset of negative emotions, learn to distract yourself, and focus your energy on more productive things. You have to try and nip it in the bud before it consumes you, for not just the rest of the day but for a week or two at a time. I have had those horrible slumps where I feel like it is never going to get any better. It is a tough place to come back from. For instance, you're sitting at your workstation and you feel the vengeful instincts rise up your throat. You have already made 86 calls and not one person has responded or even seemed interested in what you have to say, the three appointments you have already set up for that day have been a no call, no show, and you're fourth just sent you an email that said they aren't interested in coming anymore. Try your best to ignore these circumstances and focus on the work ahead of you. Switch things up and go and take a walk around the building.

Get off the phone for a while and do something productive that is different. There's no magic formula. Sometimes, you have to forcibly engage in a productive activity before your mental energies can refocus.

# 8. SPEAK UP!

Have you ever missed an opportunity to say something and then regret it for the rest of your day? Maybe you are at work in a meeting and your boss asks if anyone has any suggestions, and you have a good one, but you are too nervous to say something. Perhaps you are worried that they won't like it or think that it is probably just a bad idea. Only to then hear someone else say the very same thing or something similar to it and get all the praise. Or even perhaps walking past someone you think is attractive and making eye contact with a smile... only to let them keep on walking and not taking the time to say something to them.

You see here is the problem: We put so much energy into being worried about what people might think or how they will respond that we go through life missing opportunities. What is the worst that can happen, you engage in a conversation with that attractive person to find out they are already in a relationship? Guess what, if you speak to them and don't get a date out of it, you aren't going to get one by just walking by either. The only thing that could change is you get a date out of it. The same thing goes for the office. If you have a good suggestion, you need to share it with the group. If you do this one of two things is going to happen. They are either going to tell you why that won't work and appreciate your input, or they are going to say, "Wow what a great idea!"

We tend to be our own worst enemies. We get so caught up in worrying if someone will like what we have to say or shoot it down. Will they think better of me for suggesting it, or are they going to feel like I don't belong here? We play so many scenarios in our head that we miss the opportunity when it is right in front of us. Sure we need to be cautious of what you are going to say, but not to the point that we are missing the opportunity altogether.

When you are at work the next time, and the opportunity arises, make sure you speak up and don't be afraid to show that you are nervous about what it is you are about to share. We are all human, but without the suggestions of our teams, we may be missing something because of what we are holding back.

Showing that you are nervous means that you realize you are stepping out of your comfort zone, but also that you have given a lot of thought into the topic you are communicating about. I can almost assure you that your managers or even your subordinates aren't going to think less of you, if you are genuinely trying to make a suggestion that can make things better. If the suggestions don't work, or wouldn't be able to be applied, they will let you know. Often that suggestion could be the very thing needed to look at a problem from a different angle. This allows for a discussion to develop which tends to lead to better outcomes. For that reason alone, it is worth speaking up.

Let's stop missing opportunities because we are worried about someone else and engage in them when we have the chance. I can assure you it is almost never as bad as the thoughts we have come up with in our heads.

# 9. ANTICIPATE REJECTION

Now I have to be honest with you. When you start to speak up, you will notice that you might face rejection every now and then, which is to be expected. Have ever heard of the Law of Averages? The Law of Averages basically means that the more you try, the better your chances are at being successful. However, it doesn't mean that you won't be rejected. Just consider that eventually you will get it right, make that sale, make that amazing suggestion at work, or get that attractive person's phone number. I mean *really* think about it, if you were expecting to get it right every time you opened your mouth, you would never shut up, but neither would anyone else. So instead of expecting it to always go in your favor, make sure to change your mindset to anticipate the rejection in a situation.

As long as you are willing to take the opportunities when they present themselves, you might face rejection, but your chances of success are also much higher now. When you anticipate the rejection, it simply doesn't hit you as hard. You can also come up with a game plan to counteract the rejection itself. I am sure you can think of a time when you've said "no" to a salesperson and for whatever reason, they seem to always have something to say about it. They were most likely expecting the rejection and had practiced ways to overcome it.

Have you ever had a day when you were getting a lot of rejection and felt like you were just wasting your time? Change it up. Instead of making phone calls, switch to sending emails. Go pass out flyers, if it's applicable, but don't just to sit there and keep knocking yourself down. Yes the more you try, the better your chance of getting a positive response, but not at the expense of your sanity.

When it comes to business, you will be rejected more times than not. I can tell you from experience that it is not personal. I know that after you have been rejected for 7 hours straight, it is hard not to think it is. I mean do I smell? Should I change my shirt since I have sweat in it? Do I need to brush my teeth and get some gum, is my breath bad? Damn is it because I am Spanish. I have asked all of these questions myself, and 99% of the time it isn't personal. They just weren't interested or not in the market at the time for what I was trying to do business with.

Taking the time to figure out why people might reject you will give you a significant advantage in working on your responses. Being ready to respond to people's rejections will help you seem more confident and have better control of your conversations. Remember they aren't rejecting you, they are refusing the service or product you are trying to sell, or the idea you were trying to suggest, or whatever it is you are trying to get across.

# 10. HOW TO WIN AN ARGUMENT

It is important to know how to argue constructively. Accepting other people's views will allow you to communicate positively and share ideas with others without creating an argumentative situation. If you respect other people's opinions, more often than not they will respect your opinions too, even if they don't entirely agree with you. The world is caught up in stereotypes, and it's easy to assume wrong things all the time.

You don't have to always agree with what someone says. You can have a constructive discussion about your conflicting opinions, and it can be just fine. You don't need to go out of your way to force someone to believe what you believe. When people say they respect an opinion, they generally mean that they are prepared to tolerate it. To truly respect a belief, you have to imagine yourself in the shoes of someone with that belief. Understand their point of view and where they are coming from. Whether you agree with the opinion or not has nothing to do with this. If others don't feel that you respect their opinion, you can never successfully change that, and you won't be able to understand different opinions or have any willingness to do so.

Only when you show you fully respect or understand where a person is coming from will they ever truly open up to your opinion. So if you actually don't agree with an opinion or belief, that's all the more reason to learn and understand those opinions and beliefs and put yourself in those people's shoes. Because if you show no interest in getting to know a different opinion, you are not going to change it and the arguments will continue without any result.

When having a conversation, be an open-minded listener by suspending your judgment and exercising empathy. Listen with an open mind and show the other person that you are willing to be influenced by what he or she has to say. This doesn't mean that you have to agree with the speaker automatically; rather you should put yourself in the speaker's shoes and try to see the argument from the other side. If you want to be an effective listener, then get in touch with your conversation partner's perspective without coloring it with your own opinion.

Empathetic listening helps promote active conversation because it allows the listener to take into account where the conversational partner is coming from, both emotionally and regarding the basic content of his or her speech. This lets you measure what the speaker is saying and how you can present your ideas more accurately, which ultimately leads to better understanding and constructive conversation.

If you have an idea that this is where these discussions will go before you start them, it is wise to avoid any discussions with this person altogether and save your dignity and sanity. In other cases, the conversation may not get ugly, but if you think you need a break, disengage gracefully to continue afterward. Leave the door open to restart the conversation when the other person has calmed down. You can say, "we are not going to change each other's minds, so how about taking a break from the discussion and resuming at a later time." This is an excellent way to disengage, while accepting the discussion has gotten to a point where a civil dialog isn't possible.

This is a fine line to walk because you want to leave the discussion gracefully and want to leave the door open.

This could leave you vulnerable to an irritated person's accusation or teasing that you become the one who is upset and want to leave the discussion. You have to work past that and end the discussion immediately. If necessary, leave the room to get a drink or talk to someone else. If you are factual, intelligent, and honest up to this point, there is no reason for you to worry or feel humiliated after you leave the room.

Avoid the unhappiness of repeating arguments. Sometimes this can happen with the same person over and over, such as your spouse, loved ones, children, family, bosses, and colleagues. These negative arguments often have a consistent theme, a recurring bone of contention. Sometimes they can get out of hand and define your relationship with the other person. Regardless of whether the topic is the same or different, nothing seemingly gets resolved or agreed upon. The other party is often left upset, angered, feeling sidelined, or unheard. For some, it's common to leave these arguments feeling guilty, embarrassed, or blameworthy.

Our brains have a remarkable ability to think on repeat, and it can easily become habitual. For example, if you are used to arguing about the same household chores time and time again, you will find it difficult to suddenly walk into the kitchen without getting upset about the dirty dishes in the sink. You have to try to turn your mind away from the things that have been annoying you for weeks. You have argued about the same things before, and certainly you will have opportunities to argue about it again. Just give your mind a break from the unnecessary argument and give your conversation partner a break. This gives you the chance to focus on the real issues at hand and work on them.

Just imagine how much fun life would be if you were calm and relaxed through the whole conversation. When you are angry and starting a conversation, don't focus your anger toward the other person. More times than not, the things that upset us don't have to do with the other individual at all. If they didn't make you angry, try not to make it personal. It can be challenging not to make things personal. So next time you start feeling tense and angry, and you have to defend yourself, stop and consider where the conversation is heading and if possible, don't start any conversation until you know all of the information. Even if you have started the conversation, you can proudly stop the negative conversation by halting your speech for the time being. Step away from the conversation and retreat into another room or go someplace else.

The important thing here is identifying the triggers of your anger and determining how you can address the situation. Then you can face it head on without any hesitancy. If you have a problem with the anger issue, ignoring it won't make it go away. Angry conversations threaten your relationships, not only with loved ones but also with your work relationships and starting arguments when you are angry can put the other partner in a fight or flight mode. Angry conversations make the relationships fragile and oftentimes lead to an unhealthy situation both at home and at work.

Don't focus on past arguments with an individual. One of the biggest mistakes we all make in our conversations, arguments, and disagreements with loved ones and friends is bringing up past bitter arguments. How many times have you been talking to your partner or co-worker about an important issue in a pleasant voice, only to have them raise their voices and remind you about past events that happened ages ago? Or maybe you are the one who can't remain focused and constantly mention previous events.

Every time you bring up any event your co-worker or partner did in the past, it not only derails the current discussion, but it creates a lot of resentment between the two of you. Being unable to let go of past events and forgive someone means you are continually rejecting that part of them. People often make mistakes; it's a fact. If you want the healing to start, you have to learn to let go. The next time you feel the need to bring up old events, stop immediately! Again, this is a great time to use the "two second rule." For example, you start a conversation and bring up a past incident about how the incompetence of your co-worker created a mess, and you had to work extra hard to fix it. Or a discussion with a partner brings up old wounds. One thing will lead to another, and you and the other person can easily spiral off into a mindless mudslinging fest. No movement means no progress, so move on. You will find that you can have a conversation much more effectively and your partner or co-worker will appreciate it too.

The natural side effect of not conferring the real issue and repeatedly bringing up the past is that the disagreement will never get resolved. It will keep lingering on in your relationship with the loved ones or pollute the workplace. It's like an awful chronic migraine that won't leave you alone. Moreover, each time you bring it up, you won't be able to discuss the real issue. It will be buried underneath layers of past issues that also weren't solved for the same reason.

It is clear that for an active conversation, you have to remain focused on the present point. You can't keep bringing up the bitter past and expect progress in a relationship. Some of the natural outcomes of this include prevention of crucial issues being discussed, the build-up of resentment, and a total lack of real problem-solving. If you are in an argument, focus on that topic only and solve it. The quicker you can solve it the more efficient you will be to handle strong arguments.

The truth is that we have all dealt with the person that seems like they want to argue. The best advice I can give you when it comes to arguments is that the easiest way to win one is by not having it in the first place. A lot of this comes down to swallowing our pride and allowing the other person involved to have the win. Even if you know you are 100% right and they are wrong, let it go. They are clearly not in a frame of mind to even want to argue. They will probably calm down and realize that they were wrong and come to apologize to you. It is more important to save the relationship than to prove someone wrong. It doesn't make anyone feel any better, and the person that was proven wrong tends to become even more upset. Do your best to avoid the arguments and see how much better your relationships get, and how much more effectively you will communicate.

Another technique, and this one is my personal favorite, is to admit that you might be wrong. This will instantly help the other person lower their guard. If you engage the idea that you might be wrong and say something like "Wow, I never thought about it like that, I am probably wrong but..." Then continue with why you believed you were right. This allows the receiving party to accept that you have admitted that you might be wrong, but when you state your case as to why you believed it, they might realize that what you are saying is correct and admit that they were actually wrong. The goal here is to de-escalate the situation back down to a discussion. Now you can continue with the conversation and have an open dialogue instead of having a full blown argument where again someone is going to end up very unhappy.

The final technique I can help you with is genuinely trying to understand what it is they are trying to say. Actually, listen to what they are saying and use it in response to them. Remember people want to be heard and understood. It is also a great sign of respect. When you are trying not to have an argument with someone else you say to the person, "So what you are saying to me is that because of X, Y, and Z....)" use what they have just been telling you and repeat it back to them to show them that you value their opinion and are trying to see something from their point of view. You can now at this point explain that the reason you thought differently is that of X, Y, and Z.... and now you have stated your case. Again, you have brought the argument back to a discussion.

At the end of the day you don't always have to be right. Saving a relationship is more important than being right. Allow the other person to have the win if you can't calm the situation down, and always try to avoid the argument when possible.

# 11. THE POWER OF AN APOLOGY

One of the reasons that an apology is so powerful is because it exposes your vulnerability. If the apology is sincere, you open yourself up and allow that other person to see a side of you that many do not see. An apology is so much more than the words, "I'm sorry." People today have heard those two words so often that the power in the apology is often wasted. Think about how many times a day you hear those two words during your travels. When you are standing in line at the bank for 40 seconds, a manager will peak their head out from their cubical to express how sorry they are. When you are waiting at the drive-thru for your shake, and the line is extremely long, the cashier will express how sorry they are you have to wait. When you call a company over the phone, if your hold time is longer than 48 seconds, a representative will apologize for the delay and get you the help you need immediately. People hear the words I'm sorry so many times a day, it's no wonder that the power seems diminished.

Now fast forward to your partner who promised to be home at dinnertime. You prepared a great meal, and then you waited 3 hours for them to get home. Regardless if they were stuck at the office in a meeting or sitting in traffic; you feel like you just want to explode. Now again you are probably like me and everything you did today that didn't happen instantly was met with some sort of apology from those employees. Now your partner walks in the door, and guess what he is going to say next? Can you understand why this apology is often met with harsh words? Now you are angry because it is the 34th time today someone apologized to you, and you associate that with your partner. Your partner simply walked into an ambush. They were offering a legitimate apology and felt terrible for what happened. The fact that they said the same thing you heard all day was not intentional on their part. But now you are upset for that reason, and they are upset because you never gave them the chance to apologize. The fighting begins, and neither of you can completely understand why the other person screwed up again.

Looking at this situation from the outside, it is clear that one person simply associated apologies that they heard all day to another one from their partner, and the other didn't understand the power behind an apology. The way to truly use the power of the apology is to make your sorry more unique than all the others you hear each day. I can promise you that the fast food employees, bank staff, and customer service representatives on the phone are not that invested in making sure you accept their apology or not. Those apologies are more formality than sincere expressions on how they feel. Our society today is so focused on not offending anyone that we feel throwing out these lame apologies all day long somehow makes everything better for today. We become conditioned to assume that if we don't have a flawless experience, some employee is going to pop up and apologize for something. Is it any wonder that when you screw up and try to apologize, that your words are often met with sarcasm? People are getting to the point that these apologies are not even believable any longer. Business owners actually train employees to make sure that each customer is given attention when they enter a bank because they may take their business elsewhere. Standing in line for 38 seconds at the bank and three people will apologize for the inconvenience at least a few times.

The key to accessing the power of the apology is to break the pattern that we have all become accustomed to and uniquely say our apology. If you walk in the door late and say you are sorry, you are not going to get the response you are hoping for. Since you are late already, why not grab some flowers and write a small note about how you are genuinely sorry, and that you will make every effort to make sure it doesn't happen again. Taking the time on the drive home to write a small apology letter, then giving it to your partner rather than saying I'm sorry, will have much more of a positive effect. Walk in the door and tell your partner you have to show them something. Then as they come outside, give them flowers and a note that expresses your feelings and how you acknowledge that they are upset. Many times just letting the other person know that you are aware you upset them can defuse the situation instantly. Grab them by the hand and say since you were late that you two are going out to dinner to make up for the mess. There you can look into your partner's eyes and apologize all you want. This is an example of how actions definitely speak louder than words, especially when your partner has already heard the "I'm sorry" line too much today.

The goal is to make sure you are sincere and that you don't ruin an apology with an excuse. If you are three hours late for dinner, I am sure that you sent a text or a quick call to let them know you'll be late. This way when you do get home, they aren't surprised, and you can talk about what happened at work that got you home late in the first place. The secret is no secret at all. We just have to communicate.

At work, we wouldn't buy flowers for our boss or fellow employees. Things happen, and sometimes we get stuck late. Make it up with an apology and maybe lunch the next day, or when possible, allow the team to go home early another day. When we have positions where can control some aspects of the workflow, we need to take advantage of this. I am sure that when things happen at work, it isn't going to be the only time. There are always going to be deadlines and new customer orders to deal with. Constantly saying, "I'm sorry" can become old really quick. But a sincere, "I'm sorry, and I really appreciate all the hard work you put in for this organization" can go a long way. It shows that you are aware that this extra time can be affecting someone's personal life and that you are genuine in saying that you couldn't do it without them. Then make sure you hook them up with something sweet. A box of donuts the next morning can also go a long way.

If you knew in advance that taking a detour on the way home to pick up flowers would be more of an apology than the right words, common sense says you would make that move if you really were sincere. So why is it the majority of people never make that effort to go a little out of their way to apologize in a way that means more to the other person? The answer simply has to do with the ego. There is nothing else that causes people to stay stuck in a miserable routine than their ego. The ego is a very powerful defense mechanism that people are using the wrong way when it comes to an apology. If you understood how easy it was to simply let go, you would be amazed at the result and how you can turn your life around on a dime.

This battle is going on right now in someone's head who is reading this book. They just did something they feel terrible about, and rather than step up and make sure they express to the other person how they are genuinely sorry; they don't do or say anything. Instead, they bring out the bag with all the things the other person did that was wrong, and then they wave that in their face. So if they come home two hours late and are met with an angry partner, they decide to remind their partner that they were late for dinner 45 days ago. This starts the fire, and the fighting begins, and by the time the fighting is over, the person with the biggest lungs or most energy usually wins. This is not an effective way to settle this problem or make the other person feel your apology, and it is happening right now all over the world. We forgot that letting go of our ego can transform everything instantly. We do not have a clue as to how much power we really have because we feel that when we fight, we are in the best position to control the situation. Saying sorry means you are vulnerable, and when you're vulnerable, you expose your weakness to the rest of the world.

There is the problem in a nutshell. We merely believe that by saying we are sorry for something that we are allowing ourselves to appear weak, and we are no longer in control. The truth is that if you do apologize, you have so much more potential power than you could imagine. By telling the other person that you are sincerely sorry for something, you give that power to them to give back to you. Telling your partner that you are sorry, and making sure they feel that apology can open the door to them feeling comfortable enough to do the same when they make a mistake. Then that so-called power comes back to you. But what is that power anyway? It is nothing more than an illusion that your ego created. There really is no power in winning an argument. That is like saying you swallowed a bottle of poison with the hope of hurting your enemy. Let go of the ego, and you will see how those fights begin to disappear. Let go of the ego, and you will see how great it feels when your partner is genuinely hurt when they did something to upset you. Then both of you will look for ways to make each other happy, and the relationship will transform instantly. You don't need years of therapy here; you can fix it yourself by stopping the belief that you have to win every battle. In the end, you are hurting both of you, so try doing things differently and watch what happens.

This applies to both your home and work life, especially if you are in management. Late nights can be very common, tension can build up around deadlines, and we can feel overwhelmed with new customer orders while still trying to do the best for the current ones. This apology tactic means that you put yourself in the other person's shoes and that you make sure you let them know how much you value them. Just like your relationship at home is essential, so is the moral of your team. Swallow your pride and extend a sincere apology, show the proper appreciation, and watch as your team excels to new heights.

# 12. HOW TO SPEAK LIKE A LEADER

One of the greatest things my dad ever told me was, "Anyone can give an order, but not everyone knows how." I am not sure if he came up with this or if he read it somewhere himself, but it always stuck with me.

Leaders are people that lead their team through thick and thin, help them achieve business objectives, and exceed expectations. Although the term "born leader" is often mentioned, that is far from the truth. Leaders are not born, they try hard to excel at certain skills, and it takes a lot of time for a person to become a leader.

Among other things, leaders tend to have and develop likable and approachable personalities. One of the strongest traits a strong leader has is the knowledge of proper communication with people in their surroundings, both professional and personal. That is why we can learn a lot on how to become a master conversationalist from these strong leaders. Leaders apply conversation tactics every day and each time they communicate with someone. Let's discuss some of the characteristics that a strong leader tends to have.

Leaders are known for being confident, they can't afford to be unsure in anything they say or do. They are aware that they are in charge of entire teams. If they are uncertain of their words, it will reflect in what they do or say. This also affects the other people in their team and can negatively influence their confidence. Leaders are usually not easily influenced by negative emotions. Some of them will admit that they are afraid of speaking in front of a room full of people or scared that the project won't go the way they planned. However, great leaders will look like they are confident even when things go wrong. They aren't perfect but being able to admit when things aren't right is a sign of confidence.

Confidence is built with practice. The first thing that you need to get out of your brain is negative thinking and negative self-talk. Something I hear people say often is, "I don't have anything interesting to say to these people," or, "I am not good at speaking with other people." We have to stop telling ourselves negative statements about ourselves and switch it to only positive thoughts.

Always try to engage in as many social situations as possible. Your network of contacts will expand with time, and your confidence will rise accordingly. As it happens, more people will want to initiate the conversation with you first, and it will flow easier for you.

Another trait that a good leader has is honesty. They will always let you know the real situation, regardless of how bad it can look. A leader must be honest with his team in every moment, when things are going great and when the team is going through a rough patch. Why do leaders need to do this? Because they want people to trust them, and by being honest with their team members, leaders earn their team's trust.

Honesty is an advantage in any social situation. As we discussed earlier in the book, this doesn't mean that you should tell people everything that comes to your mind. It merely means that you shouldn't beat around the bush trying to tell what you think the other person wants to hear. Instead, be direct and build and cultivate an honest relationship with people from your surroundings.

A leader must show commitment and always make sure to act in a way that will ensure him and his team to reach their goals. A leader showing commitment to the team is being a team player. I am sure you can think of a time when you had a boss that wasn't afraid of getting dirty and doing the grunt work. A committed leader shows in their actions that they are there for their team. They should also defend their team in tough situations.

It's the same way you should act in social interactions. Be true to your word and don't say stuff you don't truly mean. Commit to the things you say you are going to do. If you offer your assistance to somebody, or you promise that you will come to a certain event, make sure to fulfill your promise. Don't disappoint your co-worker/friend/partner/kids and leave them hanging because you just didn't feel like helping them. It will backfire sooner than you think. Word of mouth spreads around quickly, and soon nobody in the office will see you as a trustworthy or likable leader.

Something every leader needs to focus

on is expressing their creativity. Coming up with innovative and unique solutions is what makes a leader great. Creativity is a personality trait held in high regard by most people because all of us can appreciate new ideas and creative thoughts. Be creative during your social interactions. Instead of having a boring chit-chat with your co-worker, put a twist into it and suggest some unusual topics. Aside from asking him dozens of questions about his current project, ask him about the last time he went to the movies or start a talk about his children.

Leaders know that having clear communication is a must. They always know how to say what they mean in a clear and concise way. If you have a leader in your team or you have a friend that has his own team, pay attention to how they are communicating. You will notice that they use conversation tactics offered in this book. They have proper body posture, they speak directly by addressing people with their names, and they properly articulate what they have to say while maintaining eye contact. Leaders don't feel any anxiety, which is something they learned with experience. If you often engage in social interactions, you will notice that you will also be relieved of any anxiety when it comes to talking with other people.

Respect is a must to be a great leader. There is a big difference between telling people what to do and asking people to do things for you. When we communicate with our teams, we have to understand that we cannot get our jobs done without them. When you ask someone to help you with a project, it gives them a sense of purpose. Admitting that you need their help means that you are showing them how much you value them. When someone feels important, and like they are part of the team, they tend to not only do better work but also have a better attitude towards the task. The last thing you want is your team feeling like they hate you because of how you tell them to do things for you. Make sure you are showing how much you respect them and their time for working on projects for you.

All teams will have their rough patches, but a reliable leader does their best to always have a positive attitude. They try to not let things get them down. They will make sure to learn what they can from a negative situation and make sure something like that doesn't happen ever again. Leaders try to always be confident and believe that everything will have a positive outcome.

Once again, we see that leaders have arrived at such a high position on the business ladder because they've become masters at the art of conversation. Like I mentioned before, people like to surround themselves with cheerful and positive people. The best way to find your positivity is to focus on the positive traits you have. We all have our qualities and flaws, so focus on what's best when it comes to you. Once you develop a positive attitude about yourself, it will be much easier to be positive when communicating with other people.

A leader not only has to come up with their own ideas and ways to help their team, but they also need to present their ideas in a way that will make their team want to follow them. A definite way of doing this is to display enthusiasm about the idea. This will inspire team members to accept your new idea and start applying it in current and future projects.

Enthusiasm is also necessary in social

interactions. You need to be in the moment and be present in every conversation. Don't let your eyes wander around the rooms and pay attention to what the other party has to say. Show some enthusiasm by giving a sincere compliment about a specific detail related to your conversation partner.

# 13. TIPS TO HAVE A BETTER CONVERSATION

I mentioned before that the first impression is crucial to what a person will think about you. That is why it is vital to leave a good impression during the first conversation you have with someone.

As a society, most people think that someone can be likable because of a trait they have. For example, they assume that the more attractive someone is, the more likable they can be because of their looks. Or simply because someone holds a position of power, we might automatically think that they are likable. We make judgements based only on what we see. This is as far from the truth as it can be.

We have to admit that some characteristics might contribute to a person being more likable. However, there is not much use in being handsome if you are obsessed with yourself. Narcissistic people often talk only about themselves, which is why they usually don't leave a good impression and bore people around them quickly. The good news is that there are conversational tactics that can help you leave a good impression during any conversation that you might have and help you be a better conversationalist.

We need to make sure that we are listening carefully. I know that I keep mentioning the concept of listening, but it is the one part of conversations where people tend to mess up the most. Aside from looking like you want to listen to the other party, make sure that you actually hear and listen what they have to say. It is such an important part and probably the easiest. It shows so much respect towards the other party that they will leave the conversation thinking about how awesome it was to speak with you. That is what listening does.

Also, make sure you are focusing on some of the physical signs you can use to show that you are paying attention. For example, nod your head in agreement when you think it's fitting, or motivate the other party to continue the story by asking a good question. Put your distractions away!

There are so many negative things in the world around us that we need to try to be positive and keep smiling even when we don't want to. I am sure you know people that love to complain. If we are honest, we have all been there, and I am sure you can admit to doing some of your own complaining. That is why we tend to want to hang around people that make us laugh. Try to look for those who can make us smile and cheer us up when we are down. When you are at a social event, make sure to put your worries aside and be positive. Nobody wants to be around a party pooper.

Your body language speaks volumes. We know that body language has a significant role to play in leaving a good impression. So, how can we use it to our advantage? Don't keep your arms crossed and try your best to maintain a good posture. Now let's be serious, it all depends on our environment and the audience in which we are engaging in conversation with. If I am outside on a cool night, I am not going to feel like someone that is crossing their arms has a malicious intent behind doing so. We don't have to try and be detectives and focus too much on body language. We just have to be aware of the signals we are sending out and the ones we are receiving. Your hands should be relaxed, and try to avoid holding on to something like a phone or keys. It sends a signal that you are more worried about something on your phone or trying to leave quickly. Keep good eye contact and avoid wandering around with your eyes. You want to look like you are interested in what the other party has to say.

Get in touch with the latest events. I genuinely enjoy keeping up with current global and local events because I like to be informed as to things that can affect me and my business. Plus, I have learned that the more I try to connect with people up the corporate ladder, the more I realize that the ones that are doing better than me in life are also into these things as well. Keep specific events in mind that are related to the environment in which you reside. You have to do your research. Whether you are meeting with a new client, going for a job interview, or even on that second date with someone special, you have to be informed on the specifics of certain situations.

Try to be as informed as you can. Staying up to date with news and music can always be useful when engaging in conversations. Try your best to avoid getting into touchy subjects like politics and religion when possible, especially if you are not really up to date on those topics. If you are in a conversation with someone and you do not know a lot about the subject, don't be afraid to admit that. This is when you need to focus more on listening than talking. The last thing you want to do is to pretend that you know what you are talking about with someone who actually does know. Keeping yourself informed about global events doesn't mean that you should know every piece of news. Simply make sure to know the trending events everyone is talking about, and you should be good to go.

Now let's focus on the latter point. Staying in touch with your environment and related events means that if you are at work, you should know what's going on with your co-workers. This comes down to knowing your audience. When your co-workers talk about personal things, make sure you listen. Someone having a baby in the family is a great conversation starter for months to come, as there are many stages. If someone mentions that someone is sick, ask how they are doing later on. It shows that you remember and that you care.

I had a customer call me one time and ask me if I could go and give an estimate. I let him know that I could be there tomorrow and he said "it would have to be next week. I am leaving tonight for my daughter's college graduation and wouldn't be back for a few days." The next week when we met I introduced myself and asked about the graduation. He looked at me pretty strange and asked me, "How did you know I was at my daughter's graduation?" I let him know that when we spoke the first time he had mentioned that he was going, which was why we couldn't meet the next day. He was astonished that I remembered something like that, but it was enough to show him I listened. Again, people want to know they are being listened to, and whenever you have an opportunity to make a conversation personal, you're heading in the right direction because you are connecting with people.

Asking good questions is essential. I know that I already mentioned this earlier in the book, but I want you to see the importance of it. Asking questions is probably one of the best ways to show your interest in what the other person is saying. You should make sure to find a balance, though. You don't want to be boring or make it seem like you are constantly interrupting. It's a conversation, not an interrogation.

If your conversation partner has just started what seems to be a long story, it's a good idea to ask a question every now and then. It will show him or her that you are listening to the story carefully and are really interested in what they are talking about. Get them to elaborate more on the things that really spark your interest. Remember, we love for someone to listen to us talk.

Questions are also a way of continuing the conversation. If the other party has finished talking about something, you can ask a question on the topic to hear more details about it.

If you are scared that you are troubling the other party with constant questions, don't hesitate to ask something along the lines of, "Am I boring you with my questions?" or "You can stop me anytime if I am asking you too many questions." You want to show that you are interested in this conversation but that you also respect their time.

It's important to not be rude. And by rude, I mean don't be judgmental. I'm sure that you wouldn't like someone you just met to pass judgment on your actions. You would consider it rude, and you would be right. That is why you should be polite if you and the other party have a different point of view on certain things. The best thing to do is to move the conversation in another direction and steer clear of any further discussion. Consider some of the tips that we discussed in the chapter *How to Win an Argument.* Let the other person have the win and practice swallowing your pride. In the long run it can pay off, especially if the conversation is with potential clients.

Along with avoiding being rude, honesty is a great practice. You should always be honest when talking to other people. Nobody expects you to like everything and it's perfectly reasonable to have your own opinion on things. Believe it or not, people will respect you more if you disagree politely and offer a different point of view.

Keep one thing in mind on this topic: the human mind works in mysterious ways. Being honest doesn't mean that you should say everything that comes to your mind. It just means that you can tell if you have a different opinion of something than the other party.

Here is a scenario: I had a female coworker ask me about how I liked her new hairstyle. To be honest, it wasn't my favorite, but I didn't want to be rude. Now obviously I am not going to be mean and say something rude. So I told her the truth: "I am a long hair type of guy, so naturally, I would say when it was longer I liked it more. But seeing this side of you is really nice, and you pull it off great." It's an honest answer, and I didn't have to hurt anyone's feelings.

I am sure you can see by now that compliments could have their own chapter because they are so important. We all love getting a compliment. Some people say that people don't care what you are complimenting as long as you say something nice about them. The one thing you want to make sure is not to overuse compliments. Make sure they are honest, unique, and seldom enough. Focus on a detail that you really like about a person. For example, compliment your co-worker's earrings. If the compliment is sincere, it will sound much better and will have a better effect than an insincere remark.

Compliments are the best way to start a conversation. When you meet a new customer for work, starting with a compliment helps to bring down the barriers we tend to put up when meeting someone new. These compliments don't even have to be personal about someone's attire; you can complement a nice painting on a wall or a desk piece. Even the furniture can be praised. As long as it is genuine, it can go a long way.

Using physical contact is also a great way to have better communication. It might seem weird at first, but it's actually a great way of strengthening your connection with other people. We make physical contact all the time. When we introduce ourselves, we shake hands. When we want someone to turn around, we tap them on a shoulder. Don't be afraid to use physical contact to make a connection with the other person, but be very careful to not overuse it. There are many different factors to consider. I am a Hispanic male and in my culture, we kiss on the cheek. Yes, even someone we just met. I can't just do that to anyone I meet, so I stick to handshakes and try to get a feel for the other person. I remember one time when I was working at the university in Financial Aid, and a student came in with her mom. They were from the Middle East, and her mom was in her traditional clothing, so I instantly noticed the cultural differences. When I reached out to shake her hand, she pulled back and said: "Out of respect to my husband, I cannot touch another man!" I let her know "no worries," and showed them to my office. It wasn't personal, it was just her culture, and I am no one to question her beliefs. One of the ladies in my office was also from the middle east and came up to me after the meeting and said, "She was rude." I asked her why and she said, "you didn't do anything wrong for her not to shake your hand. Some people just take things too far!" But this is the whole point! We don't know the exact frame of mind other people bring to the table, so we need to take our time in knowing others before we get comfortable in a physical way.

I have a buddy who has his own business, and one of his new hires came into his office and let him know that she felt very uncomfortable because when he came up behind her the other day he put his hands on her shoulder and it scared her. Now keep in mind that she acknowledged to him that she knows he didn't do it sexually or maliciously. But this woman had been raped less than a year ago, and it triggered her memories. This was a great example of communicating. She let him know of a problem, and he was able to see how he messed up, even it wasn't intentional.

He was pretty upset when he told me about it, but I explained to him that she was only expressing concern and not trying to pull anything. It's similar to when someone loses someone they care about to death. Many people will come to that person and put a hand on a shoulder and express their sympathy. It is perfectly reasonable, but after some time has passed, and life tends to move on, someone might put their hand on your shoulder to say hello, and it can trigger the memories again. He then admitted that certain things can trigger his PTSD from the military. The thing is that we all have to be considerate of the people we are touching, because we never know how they are going to feel about it. It is good to err on the side of caution and keep it to a minimum in the beginning.

# 14. THE HARDEST PERSON TO HAVE A GOOD CONVERSATION WITH

One of the hardest types of people to converse with is the person staring back at you in the mirror. A lot of it comes down to how well you understand your character, emotions, motivations, strengths, and weaknesses. Self-awareness helps us know who we are and what other people see in us. It also helps determine how similar or different we are from others. Emotional intelligence promotes self-awareness. Some of the advantages of being self-aware include expressing yourself, understanding others, having positive relationships, and having clarity of mind.

You can develop your self-awareness through introspection. This is all about questioning your motivations – why you act or think in a certain way. Know your strengths and weaknesses. Having a clear understanding of areas that you're weak and strong in is a significant step toward improving your self-awareness. This is important because after learning your strengths, you can seek more ways to capitalize on them. On the other hand, knowing your weaknesses can encourage you to do something about it. For instance, if you have a weakness for binge eating, and it is showing in your waistline, it may affect your self-image. This also affects your ability to speak confidently to those around you. And so, through introspection, you might be able to identify the link between your binge eating and your self-esteem issues, and perhaps cut out the binge eating and turn to healthy meals and workouts to get the body that you want. Finding out your weaknesses and strengths is a continuous process.

It is important to try new things. When you seek new experiences, you're going to learn a thing or two about yourself. Sometimes it takes a change of environment or a change of routine to gain a new perspective on your strengths, weaknesses, emotions, and overall character. Exploring new things is a way of stretching your limits and stepping out of your comfort zone.

One of the most standard methods of

seeking new experiences is traveling. When you travel, you get to meet people from different cultures, and their way of life might force you to look at yourself in a new light. Traveling also has a calming effect on your mind and can promote clarity of thought. I am not saying you need to book extravagant vacations to remote destinations around the world. God knows I have a few places on my bucket list I want to visit. I know how expensive it can be, but if you do some research, I am sure you can find some pretty amazing places you have not been to that are close to where you live. Then as you start to progress in life, you can extend the distance to where you are traveling to.

Meditation is also a great practice for increasing your self-awareness. The premise behind meditation is that achieving a calm mental state multiplies the odds of reaching your goals. The classic meditation pose is made by sitting on a firm surface and placing each foot on the opposing thigh. Then you can perform a breathing exercise that eliminates the noise from your mind. Meditation increases your ability to focus on your internal facets and thus helps you gain a clear understanding of the person that you are. There are so many different ways to meditate that you might want to try some different ones to see which one fits you best. I personally like transcendent guided meditation because I don't have enough control over letting my mind relax, and I instantly start to wander off. When I do this type of guided meditation, I have to listen to someone, which helps me control where my focus is going.

Reflect on who you are and get in the habit of taking stock of your life. This practice should be done on a daily basis. For instance, you may choose to reflect on the day's events before you sleep. This will help you identify the areas where you have performed well, underperformed, or outright tanked. It will grant you the insight to sharpen your weak areas and capitalize on your strengths.

Keeping a journal is also a must. Get in the habit of writing down the various emotional states that you go through during the day, as well as your triggers. This will help you assess your emotional nature, and more importantly, it will put a timeline to your emotional state. There is something when it comes to writing down your feelings and goals that helps you achieve it. It has been proven that people that write down their goals and plans have a much higher achievement rate than those that do not.

Ask for feedback, as much as you may not want to admit it. Sometimes people see things in you that you cannot see yourself. And so, you may want to hear what these people think about you, but be careful to ask people who have your best interests in mind, people who want to see you make progress. When you solicit people's opinions, you make yourself vulnerable because their feedback has the potential to hurt you. But you should be open-minded enough to allow criticism, as this is the only way to grow. With the right feedback, you will realize the areas you need to work on. This is something I have struggled with for years. My own self talk would tell me that if I am not getting feedback then it must mean that I am doing something wrong. I have even told my own managers that I have had in my past that I need the feedback. Even if they have to tell me something negative about my performance, I have to hear when I am also doing well. Or else I feel like I am not doing well. It is my own problem, but once I learned how to handle it and communicate it, I have had better understandings of my own self talk.

Know your emotional triggers. Emotions are merely the brain's way of trying to pass across an important message. There are certain things and events that cause the brain to activate the correlating emotion. It is critical to understand the various causes of your emotions. If you have gone through trauma, you are obviously emotionally scarred. Whenever you come across an event that is even loosely associated with the trauma you experienced, the bad emotions come rushing back. For instance, if you were once robbed on a dark road at night, you might find yourself getting anxious every time you're walking along lightless paths. Becoming aware that this anxiety is merely a warning that your brain is trying to send might help calm you down.

It is important to set boundaries, especially with the ones closest to you. You have to learn to set limits in order to develop your self-awareness. Setting boundaries is a way of respecting your time and showing people that you have goals to achieve. It regulates your behavior and guides you in the best manner possible. Setting boundaries and following through with the implementation takes courage and the support of other people. It is one of the critical things in understanding your limits.

Avoid being narrow-minded. A narrow-minded person hardly sees sense in what other people say, thus closing off any chance to expand their knowledge. However, if you want to increase your self-awareness, you must learn to open up your mind. There are various things you can learn about yourself if you're open-minded. This is critical especially when it comes to accepting parts of yourself that you consider unbecoming. With an open mind, you also get to change your way of thinking and free yourself from frustrations.

Have you ever argued with yourself? Have you ever needed to do something while you are lying in bed watching Netflix while telling yourself that you should get up and do what you need to be doing? Then there is a part of you saying that you can watch another rerun and push it off until later. We tend to argue with ourselves over the dumbest of things. I can't tell you how many arguments I have won in the shower talking to myself, or how many sales pitches I have delivered to myself, only not to follow through when the time came.

So the next time you are in the shower and arguing with yourself, or sitting on the couch watching television while you are telling yourself that you have stuff to do, tell yourself to shut-up and breathe for a second. See if you can actually stop the conversation. Think about what it is you really need to be doing. I know it sounds weird, but you have to have control over your mind. I get that you might be asking yourself about what this means, isn't your mind in control? It is the same voice that can hold us back in our careers because we are afraid of taking a chance. As someone who has dealt with weight problems and overcoming them, I can tell you that the voice inside your head telling you to not eat something is the one you want to be listening to. The voice that is telling you to eat one more bowl of cereal late at night is the one that got me into the weight problem to begin with. So, tell yourself to shut up and gain control of your mind before you have your next self-talk conversation.

# 15. CONCLUSION

All things must come to an end, and a good conversation is one of them. Even the best conversations can end in awkward silence, but there are ways to keep that awkward parting from happening, and the best way to do this is by being aware of the situation.

Most people use body language to show that they're ready for the conversation to end. They may increase their physical distance, look around the room, or check their watch. They may also put their jacket on or see through their handbag for their keys. This doesn't mean they're bored with you or with the conversation, just that they feel it should come to an end.

When this happens, wait for a short pause and offer a handshake. Look them in the eye and tell them how much you've enjoyed speaking with them. You might say something like, "I really enjoyed our conversation. I'll see you later," or "It's been great talking to you, but I have to go. I'll talk to you later." Whatever you say, keep it polite and friendly, and make sure you smile. Smiling always represents a friendly gesture, and it helps to show that you really mean what you say.

I can't stress this enough, please focus more of your energy on how you are listening to people. Being a good listener is the most crucial part of a good conversation. It will make people want to speak and do business with you. When you get the opportunity to get personal with someone use it to your advantage it usually opens up some great conversation topics for later on down the road.

Make sure to pause when speaking with people and use the 2-second rule. It will allow you to control your conversations better and keep your foot out of your mouth. Don't expect to master this overnight. You have, and you will notice that sometimes you will pause and go completely blank. It is all part of learning this, but the more you do it, the easier it will be and the faster you will get at thinking.

Don't hold yourself back any longer. Make sure to speak up and take advantage of the opportunities to speak when you have them. It will increase your chances of success if you just try and speak up.

Make sure you compliment people on a regular basis. And please, make it genuine. This will make them feel good and lower their guard. This is when you can make better conversations and ultimately have better business meetings and sales from your conversations.

Be kind to people. Show them that you care. There is already enough negativity in the world. Make sure to add as much positivity as you can. Go out there and speak with as many people as you can. Connect on a personal level when you can. We are all human. Allow your conversations to help you with your success for years to come.